invite
PRESS

Dynamite
Prayer

Dynamite Prayer

A 28 Day Experiment

Rosario Picardo and Sue Nilson Kibbey

invite PRESS
Plano, Texas

Contents

WEEK 3: HOLY SPIRIT POWER

WEEK 4: HOLY SPIRIT: OUR POSTURE

All royalties from the sale of this 28-day guidebook will go to the Bishop Bruce Ough Innovation Center at United Theological Seminary in Dayton, Ohio— a new holy innovation itself dreamed and birthed through breakthrough prayers for new God possibilities.

Foreword

I remember it was the beginning of 2020, shortly before the COVID-19 pandemic unexpectedly arrived. United Theological Seminary in Dayton Ohio, the place I was serving at the time, had reached a crossroads and had decided to schedule a strategic planning retreat to see if we might identify next new steps for future growth. This retreat was intended to be a large event with trustees, faculty, staff, plus a number of alumni and current students in attendance. The facilitator we enlisted was my good friend and colleague, the Reverend Sue Nilson Kibbey.

Sue is great at facilitating conversations and helping lead groups of leaders. However, something that sets Sue apart from others is her passion and reliance on prayer. I had already deployed what she calls her breakthrough prayer training in my own church by incorporating an ongoing "Breakthrough Prayer Initiative"—when the church prays in unity a crafted prayer asking God to open new doors with new possibilities at a certain time every day—and had witnessed the Holy Spirit unleash miracles in response. God must love that type of prayer!

In the same fashion, Sue suggested that United's retreat attendees also embrace a short preparatory breakthrough prayer each day for the six weeks prior to the retreat, asking God to reveal new possibilities in order to prepare our hearts, minds, and spirits for this important gathering. What might happen if we all prayed thus together daily, asking to be shown God's next ideas rather than just our own? As United's Dean of the Chapel, I worked closely with Sue to discern the scripture verse theme for our time together.

The Lord gave us 2 Timothy 1:7: "God has not given us a spirit of fear, but of power and of love and of a sound mind" (NKJV). It became clear that in this verse was something specific on which the Lord wanted us to focus: the word *power*. Sue mentioned that the significance of that word as written in the original Greek language of the New Testament, *dunamis*, is where we get the English word *dynamite*. This Greek word describes the supernatural power only God can provide in and through us and that we see manifested again and again throughout the New Testament. It was God's dunamis power, scripture reports, that resurrected Jesus from the dead. In fact, the Greek word *dunamis* is used more than one hundred twenty times from the book of Matthew through Revelation.

As we all engaged in the daily short prayer for six weeks prior to the strategic planning retreat, we were all spiritually listening as we collectively asked God to break through with new ideas and possibilities for the seminary we loved. And as difficult as this might be to believe, after the day-and-a-half retreat together and all speaking what we'd heard from God through our season of preparatory breakthrough prayer, more than five hundred distinct potential ideas had been named for the seminary's future!

For example, one of the ideas God spoke to us clearly was the need for our school to develop new partnerships. As we all continued to pray onward during the next several months after the retreat, we watched in amazement as our entire seminary became flooded with partnership opportunities and new invitations to work with incredible thought leaders and organizations. Looking back on it later, everyone who attended acknowledged the spiritually pivotal nature of the retreat and how it impacted the extraordinary new momentum forward at United Theological Seminary—and we remembered that it all started with prayer. We were tapping into God's miraculous dunamis power.

Our prayer and hope for this devotional is that, likewise, God would speak to you in new ways, that you would experience God's presence like never before, and that you would become a vessel both ignited and guided anew by the dunamis power of God's Spirit. And for what is happening at United as we've continued the breakthrough prayer, check out United president Rev. Dr. Kent Millard's afterword at the end of this resource!

Rosario Picardo

December 2021

Introduction

What is "breakthrough prayer"?

If you are seeking to follow Christ, it is crucial to prioritize time for intentional learning from and listening to the voice of God's Spirit for guidance.

If you don't, you'll only be guessing on your own about the best route to take through each day, and which decisions and choices might accomplish God's purposes in and through you. Likely you will miss living into all the fullness God has for you that is available through the Holy Spirit's dunamis that opens new doors of miraculous possibilities in the potential of any and every moment. *Dunamis* is the New Testament's original Greek word for the resurrection power of God's Spirit, and it is the core concept we hope you learn through this guidebook. When we pray, it's an opportunity to ask God's Spirit to break through and transform our lives and our world. In fact, our English word "dynamite' gains its origin from this Greek word.

Many faithful Christians develop good habits of regularly spending time reading the Bible and reflecting on scripture's life applications. Many ask God through prayer to heal, to comfort, to protect, to provide, and to bless loved ones and themselves. Yet many often say they long to understand prayer more and for their prayers to have more impact.

The purpose of this book is to show you how, through a 28-day breakthrough prayer experiment, you may become part of God's dunamis activity in the world, to live into all the explosive richness of God's intentions for you! The key in our experience is what happens when you include one more additive component in your recurrent prayer practice through each day. We call it a breakthrough prayer, asking for God's new possibilities to break through, inviting God the Almighty to open new doors, and along with it, your commitment that you'll surrender all you are now to make room for all God longs to unfold. Then notice the new eyes and ears of discernment you'll gain as you're truly led forward on the miraculous open road of faith.

Do you suppose that the Holy Spirit has always been unfolding divine responses to your prayers, imbued with the dunamis God's Spirit can provide—but you have missed it because after praying, you resumed preoccupation with allowing your own preferences and opinions to guide your way? Shift away from assuming you're finished when your prayer time ends. Go forward with your day, certainly. But now in every next moment following your prayers of any length, continue to keep your heart and spirit expectantly receptive, ready to notice and follow God's unfolding response and guidance.

How to use this guidebook

This *Dynamite Prayer* devotional is a prayer-saturated 28-day guidebook to help you begin to experiment by incorporating the addition of a surrendered breakthrough-prayer practice into your daily life following Christ, and to help you cultivate your capacity to discern, to notice, to respond to God's guidance, and to live by the miraculous power of the Spirit.

Each day's entry is divided into five key parts:

- A scripture **reading** that emphasizes God's dynamic (dunamis) power.

- A personal devotional **insight** about some unique aspect of the Holy Spirit.

- **Prompts** to assist you in cultivating your own honest and authentic reflection, journaling, or discussion with others.

- A short breakthrough **prayer** to keep your mind and heart aligned and focused God-ward throughout the day. There's also space for you to craft your own breathrough prayer as well!

- An even shorter targeted breakthrough prayer version that we've nicknamed a **prayer-hold**, which is a style of prayer practiced throughout our historic Christian faith.

At the end of each day's devotion, we have provided inspiration from a sister or brother in Christ about the dynamic power and activity of God's Spirit.

About **prayer-holds**: A prayer-hold is a short phrase or word from a scripture verse you can use for frequent prayer use throughout the day. Every hour (or whenever you become aware that you are feeling inadequate, uncertain, or tempted to slide off track spiritually) you can simply pray the day's short prayer-hold. This helps you refocus and realign your spiritual eyes back on discerning and following the Spirit's activity and guidance.

Examples of short scripture-based "prayer-holds" could be:

God is faithful.
From 1 Thessalonians 5:24 (CEB): "The one who is calling you is faithful and will do this."

Lead me to the rock that is higher than I.
From Psalm 61:2

Or even single-word prayer-holds from scripture are useful. Here's one such example:

Finish.
From Philippians 1:6 (CEB): "the one who started a good work in you will stay with you to complete [finish] the job by the day of Christ Jesus."

To use the day's prayer-hold, set a reminder on your watch or phone or make a written note to pause, refocus, and pray this prayer-hold at convenient moments throughout the day, such as hourly, at meals, or another schedule that will assist you best.

Once you've completed your 28-day Dynamite Prayer guidebook, our hope is that you will find that it has become a ready reference to which you can return again and again for refreshing yourself. Keep your breathrough prayer experiment going.

Note that this guidebook is also designed for group use. Use this devotional to connect with others who are navigating their own 28-day dunamis experiment, so that you have spiritual companions with whom to discuss, share, encourage and pray along the way. You can celebrate your breathrough together. You may consider using this guidebook at your church as the basis of a congregation-wide 28-day Dynamite Prayer experiment of breakthrough prayer and spiritual growth together. Your pastor could preach a sermon series at the same time, based on each of the four weekly dunamis themes named in the contents. What powerful spiritual momentum this could create!

Finally, be confident that as you pray each day, God's power—the supernatural, resurrection dunamis power of Christ—will break through, fill you, and guide you beyond what you could ever ask, think, or imagine (Ephesians 3:20). Let your prayer experiment now begin.

Day 1: Overshadowing

The angel answered, "The Holy Spirit will come on you, and the power [dunamis] of the Most High will overshadow you. So the holy one to be born will be called the Son of God."
—Luke 1:35

Insight

The story in today's verse, historically referred to as the Virgin Birth and Incarnation, remains timelessly relevant. That's because in it we observe an example of what occurs when we surrender ourselves to the birth of God's miraculous new creation within. In our finite minds it is difficult to comprehend God becoming a human being and the Holy Spirit helping Mary conceive Jesus. Luke recorded that, according to the message of the angel for Mary, a miracle beyond her comprehension would occur because "the power [dunamis] of the Most High will overshadow you."

Mary surrendered by responding, "I am the Lord's servant. May your word to me be fulfilled."

In our society today, the word *overshadow* might infer a negative connotation of subservience or getting sidelined from the limelight. However, in the original Greek language in which Luke wrote this account, the word translated into English for us as "overshadow" was used only five other times in the New Testament. It depicts a shining cloud, surrounding and enveloping with brightness. Its use here points back to the Old Testament, where God's people were guided by a bright pillar of cloud by day and an equally vivid pillar

1

of fire by night. In essence, it evidences the immediate presence and power of God.

Consider the prospect that God's Spirit longs to uniquely overshadow you anew today with the miraculous creative brightness of dunamis power and presence. Will you choose to accept the invitation, to become willing to surrender your own plans and preferences and thus make room—like Mary?

Prompt

How comfortable—or uncomfortable—is spiritual surrender for you? What do you sense needs be surrendered into God's care this moment, so that you have room to receive a new overshadowing of the Spirit's dunamis? Write it here.

My Breakthrough Prayer for Today

God, may your Holy Spirit's power overshadow my mind, thoughts, will, and agenda for what you desire to birth anew in me, through me, and around me. Amen.

Or craft your own breakthrough prayer below.

Prayer-Hold (to pray throughout today)

God, overshadow me . . .

[Fill in the rest of the sentence with your greatest need today].

To move from the mundane to the magnificent, we have to allow God's love to overshadow us.
—Callie Picardo

Day 2: The Wilderness

Jesus returned to Galilee in the power [dunamis] of the Spirit, and news about him spread through the whole countryside.
—Luke 4:14

Insight

Have you had more experiences in what seemed like the wilderness, the deserts, and the valleys of life than on the mountaintops? Mountaintop experiences are monumental. You feel on top of the world. Perhaps you have experienced a mountaintop spiritual moment in your life, such as while going to retreats or conferences or while attending a church worship service.

Sometimes, though, it feels like you face more valleys than mountaintops The "valley" is when you get knocked down and everything is stripped away. As difficult as it is, a valley is also sacred: it is in the valley when you have cause to reflect on your own deep sense of inadequacy. In those moments, you realize you can't do it all, you are finite, and you are in desperate need of God's redemptive grace and power.

Think back on valleys in your life. As you remember those times, you may recognize now how God's assistance helped you through. This is the potency of God's dunamis power. As described in the scripture passage that includes today's verse, Jesus went through an extreme set of temptations out in the wilderness—forty days of solitude, denying his flesh while also being hungry, exhausted, and coerced by the devil to take the easy way out. We read that after Jesus overcame the temptations, he had finally become ready to emerge and return to start his public ministry. But Jesus only overcame the devil's temptations through "the power of the Spirit." More specifically, dunamis resurrection-strength power came upon him when he chose to reject taking the easy way out. When he arrived back in Galilee, he was empowered to bring a new miraculous presence and impact.

Real power comes not from your own strength or simply the power of positive thinking. Miraculous power, dunamis power, flows through when you reject what is the easy route in favor of saying yes to what you know of God's preferred future for you.

Prompt

What temptation (of any kind) faces you today—and what choice do you sense you need to make for the empowerment of God's dunamis to flow? Write it here.

My Breakthrough Prayer for Today

God, break through with your dunamis power in all my choices to accomplish your highest good. Amen.

Or craft your own breakthrough prayer below.

Prayer-Hold (to pray throughout today)

God, in the Spirit's dunamis I say yes to your future.

The value of consistent prayer is not that He will hear us, but that we will hear Him.
—William J. McGill

Day 3: Sent

When Jesus had called the Twelve together, he gave them power [dunamis]
and authority to drive out all demons and to cure diseases, and he sent them
out to proclaim the kingdom of God and to heal the sick.
—Luke 9:1–2

Insight

After Jesus' temptations in the wilderness, he entered three years of earthly ministry empowered with the dunamis of God's Spirit to serve, minister, and heal. Likewise, when Jesus sent out those whom he had chosen to be his disciples, he blessed them with the same miraculous dunamis power for mission and service on behalf of God's people. He also sent them out with the responsibility, or authority, to act and minister on his behalf and according to his directions.

The supernatural power given to those early disciples was a foretaste of what they would experience post-resurrection on the day of Pentecost.

As a disciple of Jesus, you too are sent out with this very same power through the Holy Spirit that raised Christ from the dead and was poured out on his early followers. And you too are charged with the responsibility to live under God's authority as you go forward into each day to serve the needs of others on Christ's behalf.

Christians often desire and even pray for God's blessings, hoping for self-serving material benefits or financial gain. Yet the miraculous dunamis resources a disciple of Jesus receives also include the responsibility alongside to leverage everything for God's good, not to hoard personally. What does that look like? Signature characteristics of living responsibly under God's authority include your prayer-fueled alignment with the Holy Spirit who will provide you spiritual protection when facing temptation, plus dunamis-inspired direction in times of uncertainty.

Life following Jesus is far more than a pursuit of wealth, acclaim, knowledge, and blessings. As the Twelve did, surrendering to receive the Spirit's dunamis power and living obediently under God's authority and direction will provide fulfillment beyond what you can ask, think, or imagine.

Prompt

Under whose authority would you honestly say you live and act—your own, someone else's, or God's? What would you need to reconsider to make God's dunamis-infused authority your foundation today? Write it here.

My Breakthough Prayer for Today

God, may the Holy Spirit break through any selfish habits or fears so that I may be an instrument of your dunamis power and authority sent into today. Amen.

Or craft your own breakthrough prayer below.

Prayer-Hold (to pray throughout today)

Sent with God's power and authority.

We must alter our lives in order to alter our hearts, for it is impossible to live one way and pray another.
William Law

Day 4: Unbelief

Coming to his hometown, [Jesus] began teaching the people in their syna-
gogue, and they were amazed. "Where did this man get this wisdom and
these miraculous powers?" they asked. "Isn't this the carpenter's son? Isn't
his mother's name Mary, and aren't his brothers James, Joseph, Simon and
Judas? Aren't all his sisters with us? Where then did this man get all these
things?" And they took offense at him. But Jesus said to them, "A prophet is
not without honor except in his own town and in his own home." And he
did not do many miracles [dunamis] there because of their lack of faith.
—Matthew 13:54–58

Insight

"This is the way it's always been and will never change." Have
you ever heard or observed a similar attitude in your family, your
friends, your coworkers—or even noticed it in yourself?

A perspective that assumes change for the better is impossible,
even if it's desired, and inhibits openness to new potential God-
designed solutions. That's exactly what Jesus faced during his earthly
ministry when he returned to his hometown to preach and teach
the good news of God's kingdom. He had spent forty days in the
wilderness under heavy temptation and had not taken the easy way
out. Later, he was back in the area where he had lived all his life,
dunamis-endowed, to lead and deliver a new miraculous ministry.
Yet those who had previously known Jesus now refused to view him
through different eyes of hope-filled faith. Instead, they clung to
their unbelief that anything could change.

As a result, today's scripture indicates that the resurrection
power dunamis available to flow through Jesus on their behalf
was decreased. The original Greek word that's been translated into

English as "unbelief" in this passage literally means "faithlessness"— or a lack of trust in the God of promise.

It's not possible to control others' level of trust in God's ability, but what about your own? A life lived with continual faith-filled confidence in the supernatural dunamis activity of the Holy Spirit creates space for its potential flow in and through you via your prayer life. Beware of any type of faithless resignation about "what is," and choose instead to view everything and everyone with potential for God's transformation—including yourself. The same power by which Jesus rose from the dead continues alive and active now.

Prompt

Assess yourself honestly. Have you assumed an attitude of unbelief in any aspect of the overall fabric of your faith that limits the God potential that you might otherwise see in yourself, those around you, or your current situation? Has this self-limited what the Holy Spirit might desire to do? Write it here.

My Breakthrough Prayer for Today

God, may your Holy Spirit replace my eyes of unbelief with your eyes of dunamis possibilities. Amen.

Or craft your own breakthrough prayer below.

Prayer-Hold (to pray through today)

New eyes . . .

Prayer breaks all bars, dissolves all chains, opens all prisons, and widens all straits by which God's saints have been held.
—*Edward McKendree Bounds*

Day 5: Ability

Again, it will be like a man going on a journey, who called his servants and entrusted his wealth to them. To one he gave five bags of gold, to another two bags, and to another one bag, each according to his ability [dunamis]. Then he went on his journey. The man who had received five bags of gold went at once and put his money to work and gained five bags more. So also, the one with two bags of gold gained two more. But the man who had received one bag went off, dug a hole in the ground and hid his master's money.
—Matthew 25:14–18

Insight

Jesus told a parable to his followers, and today's scripture passage is the first portion of the story. He explained that each servant had been blessed with an allotment of dunamis, sometimes translated in our English New Testament as "ability," for the purpose of accomplishing the master's work. The first two servants did indeed use their God-given abilities through successful efforts to prosper and increase the master's resources they had been given. The third servant also received a portion of the master's resources but instead took a far different course of action. Rather than also stepping out with an attempt to multiply its usefulness, he buried it and went on about his own business. Jesus explained at the end of the parable that upon his return the master was pleased with the first two, but the third lost everything he had been given.

Like the servants in the parable, if you have said "yes!" to new life in Christ, you are are also equipped with a special portion of God's miraculous dunamis. It manifests as your unique ability or giftedness to participate and multiply in the Spirit's work of bringing Christ's good news through various redemptive expressions of love and kindness into the lives and the world around you. This is more than simply your own natural human talent or ability. Your new life in Christ has also infused you with a unique dose of the Holy Spirit's supernatural capability.

Also like the servants in the parable, you have a decision to make: Will you apply this miraculous God-given ability outward, or will you bury it and focus only on your own affairs? Will you use your time each day as your own, or will you recognize it as available for the Holy Spirit's guidance to deploy you to serve—whether in highly visible settings or in small unobserved actions for good?

Prompt

What unique dunamis, or gifting of ability by God, have you been given, at least according to your own self-awareness? Write it down. What shift in spiritual availability and flexibility would better honor and multiply the impact of your supernatural dose of gifting on behalf of those around you? Write it here.

My Breakthrough Prayer for Today

God, break through any resistance in me to invest and multiply your gifts of dunamis. May I become like the first servant in the scripture. Fill me with confidence, eagerness, and willingness to be used for your greater purposes. Amen.

Or craft your own breakthrough prayer below.

Prayer-Hold (to pray through today)

Use me . . .

True prayer is not a mental exercise or a vocal performance. It goes deeper than that - it is a spiritual transaction with God.
—Charles Spurgeon

Day 6: Wait Training

I am going to send you what my Father has promised; but stay in the city until you have been clothed with power [dunamis] from on high.
—*Luke 24:49*

Insight

Americans are the most time-conscious people in the world. We are always in a hurry. We invented fast food, instant coffee, instant messenger, express mail, express oil changes, and expressways.

We hate to wait for . . .

- the long line at the grocery store, even if we're in the self-checkout line.
- the customer service person to pick up the call when we've been placed on hold.
- a reply to a text message when we're deep in conversation.
- a friend who is chronically late.
- traffic jams, especially when we're headed somewhere important (which is seemingly always).

We detest waiting for things that don't mean a whole lot to us in the long run. But what about those things that are of greater importance?

- waiting for that adoption to go through.
- waiting to have the surgery that was scheduled or lab results from the doctor.
- waiting for direction in our lives. What's next?

As much as we hate waiting, something supernatural and powerful can happen in the waiting. Waiting is not for the faint of heart. "Wait training" will build spiritual muscles of faith we never knew we had to help get us to a level we never thought we could achieve.

After his resurrection, Jesus appeared again to his disciples. They were overjoyed to see him, and that's when Jesus gave them a final problematic assignment before he ascended into heaven: to wait. Jews had already been waiting for countless years for the Messiah to come the first time. Now the one they had waited for was leaving, and they had to wait . . . again?

And now to you personally. Does God have you in a wait training program? Perhaps waiting isn't just the hold period but part of your journey with Christ. Maybe the waiting is just the moment you need to give up your impatience and embrace the process of the Holy Spirit's dunamis to strengthen your muscles of faith.

Prompt

What happens when you find yourself waiting on God? What is your default response? Consider new ways to increase your "spiritual muscles" while waiting on God so that the Holy Spirit's dunamis has opportunity to continue to mature and transform you rather than taking matters into your own hands. Write it here.

My Breakthrough Prayer for Today

God, help me see my seasons of waiting as open doors through which I can connect with you rather than as frustratingly closed doors to my own desires. Amen.

Or craft your own breakthrough prayer below.

Prayer-Hold (to pray throughout today)

Wait for God's dunamis . . .

> *Waiting in prayer is a disciplined refusal to act before God acts.*
>
> —*Eugene Peterson*

Day 7: Timing

But you will receive power [dunamis] when the Holy Spirit comes on you;
and you will be my witnesses in Jerusalem, and in all Judea and Samaria,
and to the ends of the earth.
—Acts 1:8

Insight

Staying alert for God's timing and open doors has been a theme in the lives of many throughout the Bible. The beauty of "wait training," as we outlined yesterday, is that one day, the wait is over, and there is an after. Consider:

- After long years of building the ark in a drought, Noah finally felt the first drop of rain.

- Long after God had promised Abraham that he would start a great nation, he finally became a father.

- After four hundred years of slavery, Moses finally was given an opportunity at Pharaoh's throne to free the children of Israel.

- Following fourteen years unjustly inprisoned after being betrayed by his brothers, Joseph was finally elevated to second-in-command in Egypt.

- After waiting and watching for the opportune moment, Queen Esther could finally act to save her people.

- After waiting on God while she cared for Naomi, Ruth finally was granted God's provision through Boaz.

19

- After waiting a lifetime of sixty to seventy years, Job was finally vindicated.
- After thirty years, Jesus was finally unleashed to start his earthly ministry.

As told in the first chapter of Acts, the disciples gathered in the upper room at Jerusalem and continued in "wait training" until the arrival of the Holy Spirit.

It matters what we are doing until God's response and timing unfolds. And in Acts we read that the disciples were not passively, but actively, waiting:

- They were in the right place.
- They prayed while they were waiting.
- They were patient and persistent while they were waiting.
- They didn't complain while they were waiting.
- They didn't throw in the towel while they were waiting.
- They didn't wait alone. They waited together.

It was worth the wait. Not too long after, the dunamis power of the Holy Spirit was poured out upon the witness of the disciples and the early believers for what became a new growing movement that would change the face and future of the world—including our own lives today.

Prompt

Of the biblical individuals listed in today's "Insight" section, to which can you most relate? Pause and invite God's Spirit to bring to your memory an occasion or situation when God's timing and provision showed itself, in hindsight, to have been far better than what you had thought you wanted. Write it here.

My Breakthrough Prayer for Today

God, break through my urgency to do or speak my way, and instead to surrender and wait for the dunamis of the Holy Spirit to open doors, provide, direct, guide, and empower me. Amen.

Or craft your own breakthrough prayer below.

Prayer-Hold (to pray throughout today)

Come, Holy Spirit . . .

Nothing happens in the Kingdom of God unless it is preceded by prayer.
—John Wesley

Day 8: "Power" Charge

[...that you may know] his incomparably great power [dunamis] for us who believe. That power is the same as the mighty strength he exerted when he raised Christ from the dead and seated him at his right hand in the heavenly realms.
—Ephesians 1:19–20

Insight

Our second week in discovering breakthrough prayer focuses on increasing awareness of what you can expect of the power of God's Spirit.

Consider this analogy. Have you ever left home without taking along your laptop, tablet, or phone charge cord? When the battery of your device eventually runs low, your ability to be productive becomes compromised or even comes to a stop. Likely you pay careful attention to packing your charge cords to keep your electronic devices powered so your interactions, connections, and work can continue uninterrupted.

The apostle Paul wrote a heartfelt letter to Christians in Ephesus, which is included in the New Testament. Today's scripture verse, which comes from that letter, includes part of his prayer for the people of Ephesus about staying connected to their source: the Spirit's dunamis power. He emphasized that what God's Spirit provides to power up Christ followers is the identical resurrection-strength power by which Jesus rose from death on the cross to life.

How often do you try to accomplish following Jesus using your own human strength, coming up with your own solutions, and applying your own wisdom and best efforts before finally turning to God? Whatever "power" of your own eventually fails without actively staying plugged in to your one and only true Holy Spirit dunamis power source.

Attending an hour-long worship service in person or online each week isn't enough to become and stay fully spiritually charged, just as quickly skimming over this devotional entry each day before moving on to the tasks of your to-do list is not enough. What will connect or reconnect you to a supernational dunamis power charge right now? Take time to pause, reread, and reflect upon the scripture. Then silence your inner dialogue of thoughts to find spiritual stillness before God. Offer all that's simmering in your heart to the Almighty in prayer, either with words spoken aloud or silently spoken in your heart. Then invite God to break through, open new doors of possibility, and lead you afresh as you look up and out with expectancy going forward. See what the Holy Spirit's dunamis will then show, provide, and accomplish.

Prompt

Upon what sources do you typically find yourself relying to power you through the day, if they are sources other than your faith or prayer? (Examples might be what you believe you learned through past experiences, your education, previous expertise, your senior status, your youthfulness, physical energy, your financial wealth, a role or position you hold, or others). Has one of these alternate power sources failed you or steered you wrong? What did you learn? Write it here.

My Breakthrough Prayer for Today

God, break through my mistaken confidence in my own limited "power." Show me new ways to invest myself in your spiritual power. Help me to connect more continually with your Spirit. Amen.

Or craft your own breakthrough prayer below.

Prayer-Hold (to pray throughout today)

God's mighty strength is my power . . .

> *If we are ever free from the sense of need [to pray], it is not because the Holy Spirit has satisfied us but because we have been satisfied with as much as we have.*
> *—Oswald Chambers*

Day 9: "Power" Prayer for Others

I pray that out of his glorious riches he may strengthen you with power [du-namis] through his Spirit in your inner being, so that Christ may dwell in your hearts through faith. And I pray that you, being rooted and established in love, may have power [dunamis], together with all the Lord's holy people, to grasp how wide and long and high and deep is the love of Christ, and to know this love that surpasses knowledge—that you may be filled to the measure of all the fullness of God.
—Ephesians 3:16–19

Insight

Throughout Paul's New Testament letters, originally composed and sent to those who were part of the early Church, he frequently noted that he was facing life-threatening persecutions and problems of his own. Yet Paul continually took the time to pray for others as he wrote. In fact, part of the final verse of today's scripture is often spoken by church leaders today as a benediction prayer for Holy Spirit dunamis power and love over the entire congregation:

"May you be filled to the measure of all the fullness of God. Amen."

Hundreds of years before Paul wrote and sent this prayer to other Christ followers whom he knew and loved, the Old Testament recounts the heartbreaking story of a man named Job. Through a series of escalating tragedies and challenges Job lost his family, his property, his wealth, and his health. Through it all, he hung on to his faith. At God's direction, he likewise moved his preoccupation off his own concerns and prayed for the well-being of his friends. After he prayed, God's miraculous healing and restoration of Job's own health and hope took place (Job 42:7–16). When we pray to God on behalf of another, we are lifting that person's life, joys, and challenges to the threshold of the Almighty's grace and miraculous dunamis power, asking God's blessings over them. As we pray, we experience God's spiritual blessing ourselves.

Perhaps right now you are in the midst of some type of personal stress and turmoil. It could be with your health, a friendship or relationship, your finances, or a difficult decision with which you are wrestling. Maybe you are experiencing painful consequences as a victim of another's actions. Whatever it might be, you likely feel drawn to center your prayer focus upon your own circumstances.

However, the Holy Spirit's dunamis power is also released through your prayers for others. And by praying for others even during your own difficult moments, you may be surprised by the impact of the Spirit's dunamis as much, if not more, for yourself.

Prompt

When you have prayed for someone else, for what do you usually pray? What new observations about how to pray for someone else did you notice in today's scripture? Who comes to mind in need of your prayers right now? Write it here.

My Breakthrough Prayer for Today

God, set me free from the limits of a self-focused prayer life. May your Spirit inspire and empower me to expand into dunamis-infused prayer on behalf of as many others as possible throughout this day. Amen.

Or craft your own breakthrough prayer below.

Prayer-Hold (to pray throughout today)

Spirit, release your power through my prayers . . .

Through the connective tissue of prayer, [Christ] cracks open the door that makes us at least a small part of how these massive plans of His are translated into the lives of people we know. Including ours.
—Priscilla Shirer

Day 10: Guides and Provides

Now to Him who is able to do far more abundantly beyond all that we ask or think, according to the power [dunamis] that works within us, to Him be the glory in the church and in Christ Jesus to all generations forever and ever. Amen.
—Ephesians 3:20–21 NASB

Insight

You may have heard the familiar saying, "Where God guides, God provides." It's true! God seems to enjoy showing off the Spirit's dunamis power through divine guidance. As Paul emphasized in his blessing found in today's scripture, God's resurrection power is capable of more than our minds can think or our words can describe when it comes to providing on behalf of where God is leading and guiding us.

Roz saw this at Mosaic Church, where he serves as copastor, when the COVID-19 pandemic hit. Like most other churches and organizations, Mosaic had to quickly pivot to change the way everything was done. The congregation could no longer meet in its rented movie theater for worship services on Sundays because the theater ceased operation. Instead, the Holy Spirit's dunamis birthed a new vision through the prayers of Mosaic's leadership for parking lot/drive-in Sunday worship services using an FM transmitter for sound, with the band and preacher placed on top of a flatbed truck and the church attendees parked at a safe distance all around. No location, equipment, or logistics had materialized as the first Sunday approached. But church leaders and congregation continued to unite in prayer and watched in amazement as God provided everything needed for not one but multiple locations for outside worship.

When the season changed and cold weather arrived, God next unexpectedly guided them to a vacant commercial department store space in a nearby mall with surprisingly low rent. But Mosaic Church would need to purchase additional equipment, accomplish renovations to the space, and raise "move-in" funds—all in the midst of the global pandemic. Church leaders continued to pray and set a financial commitment goal of $87,000. But individuals whom the Holy Spirit's dunamis empowered to step up gave nearly $100,000 in just nine days—immeasurably more than was imagined.

Perhaps you have heard of similar, personal stories of God's provision as well. Or maybe you've wished your own life could become an example of such miraculous guidance and God's supply for your needs. Be encouraged as you make prayer the surrender of your own ideas and preferences, as you make the foundation of your life following Christ, and as you invite God to lead you instead.

Whatever you ask of God in prayer, then, God hears and wisely responds. Are you worried that how God might guide and what God might provide may not be exactly what you think you want? Rest in faith and confidence that the Spirit's dunamis will guide and provide according to what God desires, according to the Almighty's divine intent and agenda of transforming, redemptive love—which always accomplishes far more than our own preferences (and will transform you in the process). Trust God's dunamis power at work in you, and find courage to move forward as your next steps appear. You'll soon be on the open road of the adventure of faith!

Prompt

Whenever you ask God's Spirit for guidance, then fully open yourself to spiritually listen and receive, you'll begin to recognize that God always responds and provides. To what extent do you believe this enough to trust and completely lean into it? Do you ever pray asking for God's provision but then don't go along with God's (potentially course-correcting) guidance as it becomes evident to you? Write it here.

My Breakthrough Prayer for Today

God, part the floodwaters of my fear that you will not always provide, as you guide and set me on the solid ground of relying on your Spirit's dunamis power. Amen.

Or craft your own breakthrough prayer below.

Prayer-Hold (to pray throughout today)

Far more abundantly . . .

> *Bold prayers honor God, and God honors bold prayers. God isn't offended by your biggest dreams or boldest prayers. He is offended by anything less. If your prayers aren't impossible to you, they are insulting to God.*
> *—Mark Batterson*

Day 11: Walk and Talk

For we know, brothers and sisters loved by God, that he has chosen you,
because our gospel came to you not simply with words but also with power
[dunamis], with the Holy Spirit and deep conviction. You know how we
lived among you for your sake.
—1 Thessalonians 1:4–5

Insight

Have you ever attended what's known as a recovery gathering? It might have been Alcoholics Anonymous (AA), or AlAnon, or Celebrate Recovery, or other similar support group. All emphasize a central focus upon the twelve steps, which are a set of spiritual principles. When practiced together as a way of life, they can loosen strongholds of all-consuming and destructive habits and enable recovery and freedom. This type of recovery is not about empty words or head knowledge. It's about action, about making the next right choice in front of you, which becomes a tangible example that others can emulate. Sharing your story of recovery to instill hope for the same in others is interwoven into a proactive recovery journey.

In the same way, the Spirit's dunamis power that is progressively transforming, maturing, and shaping the new life in Christ within you can become a bright practical example of hope for others. Give yourself permission to share your story of faith and trust in Christ with your words whenever the opportunity arises. But your words regarding your confidence in the power of prayer will be meaningless unless it is also evident through your lived-out choices, your demonstrated attitude, and your tangible acts of love toward yourself and others.

As Paul acknowledges in this scripture, the greatest demonstration and witness of God's power is the miracle of transformed lives. In Christ you are a living miracle. Far more than words or preaching, it is your life that speaks. In fact, your life surrendered through prayer to live daily as a vessel for the Spirit's dunamis to flow through you will emanate light and encouragement. As Jesus told his disciples, "Let your light shine before others, that they may see your good deeds and glorify your Father in heaven" (Matthew 5:16).

Prompt

Consider this honestly. How much of what you say (your words) matches what you actually do (your attitudes, behavior, handling of your finances and possessions, treatment of others, and time invested to grow and mature spiritually)? In what areas are you aware of your greatest mismatches? Write it here.

My Breakthrough Prayer for Today

God, I ask for your help to demolish any habits, fears, and thoughts that prevent your light from shining genuinely through me as a witness to others. Amen.

Or craft your own breakthrough prayer below.

Prayer-Hold (to pray throughout today)

God, speak and shine through my life . . .

We never grow closer to God when we just live life. It takes deliberate pursuit and attentiveness.
—Francis Chan

Day 12: God's Promises

Yet [Abraham] did not waver through unbelief regarding the promise of God, but was strengthened in his faith and gave glory to God, being fully persuaded that God had power [dunamis] to do what he had promised.
—Romans 4:20–21

Insight

We live in a time where day-to-day promises don't always mean much or are frequently broken. And with unfulfilled promises come disappointment and broken trust.

But God's way of operating is different: God has the miraculous power to deliver on God's promises. Keep in mind this assurance from Paul: "For as many as the promises of God are, in Him they are yes; therefore through Him also is our Amen to the glory of God" (2 Corinthians 1:20 NASB).

What does a "promise of God" mean? Here are a few of the many that appear throughout the Bible (these spoken by Jesus):

"Come to me, all you who are weary and burdened, and I will give you rest. Take my yoke upon you and learn from me, for I am gentle and humble in heart, and you will find rest for your souls." (Matthew 11:28–29)

"I have told you these things, so that in me you may have peace. In this world you will have trouble. But take heart! I have overcome the world." (John 16:33)

And the most important promise of all:

"For God so loved the world that he gave his one and only Son, that whoever believes in him shall not perish but have eternal life." (John 3:16)

Paul points out the faith of Abraham as an example. According to the Old Testament, Abraham moved to a land he had never visited, was promised by God that he would become the father of many nations, and was told that in old age he and his wife Sarah would have a child. None of this could have been even remotely possible through Abraham and Sarah's own strength, hopeful thinking, or optimism. It happened only by God's power delivering on God's promise. God established a promise of redemption and renewal long before Jesus' disciples received their promise of dunamis empowerment by the Holy Spirit to take the good news of Jesus to the world.

Prompt

Have you said yes to God's promise of new eternal life through believing in Jesus as your Savior? Are there other promises of God in scripture that you hold closely to your heart and through which you have received peace, assurance, hope, guidance, or deliverance? If yes, which one(s)? Write it here.

My Breakthrough Prayer for Today

God, shift any stubborn no in me regarding the promises you offer so that through your dunamis power I may experience their yes in you. Amen.

Or craft your own breakthrough prayer below.

Prayer-Hold (to pray throughout today)

God's promises, God's power . . .

The future is as bright as the promises of God.
—William Carey

Day 13: Dunamis Wisdom

For since in the wisdom of God the world through its wisdom did not know him, God was pleased through the foolishness of what was preached to save those who believe. Jews demand signs and Greeks look for wisdom, but we preach Christ crucified: a stumbling block to Jews and foolishness to Gentiles, but to those whom God has called, both Jews and Greeks, Christ the power [dunamis] of God and the wisdom of God. For the foolishness of God is wiser than human wisdom, and the weakness of God is stronger than human strength.
—1 Corinthians 1:21–25

Insight

God's Spirit-infused wisdom is often very different than the "wisdom" of the world. Jesus was a teacher with profoundly supernatural wisdom, offering a spiritual depth unlike anything anyone had ever heard before. Though highly educated religious dignitaries often tried to trip him up with their questions and also rejected his answers, Jesus consistently spoke and exemplified the power (dunamis) of wisdom from God.

After Jesus' death and resurrection, the early Christian church grew. With the gospel widely proclaimed, leaders like Paul were imprisoned for likewise speaking God's wisdom and truth about the miracles and message of Christ crucified. When Paul wrote his first letter to the Corinthian Christian church, he included the sentences of today's scripture. Clearly, he wanted all followers of Christ to understand that seeking God's wisdom is far superior to the world's.

What about you? Do you ever have moments in which you feel lost or uncertain, even as others around you offer you their well-meaning personal advice about your circumstances or challenges? God desires to give us the Spirit's dunamis-inspired wisdom for the situations we face, the direction we need to go, and the decisions we need to make. The pathway to receiving God's wisdom is accessible through spending time reflecting on scripture and through praying—emptying yourself of your own assumptions or others' advice—and then connecting with God to ask, listen, and receive.

Praying to request God's miraculous wisdom is not seeking the easy solution, a quick fix, or validation of what makes the most worldly sense to you. Instead, it's asking for God's dunamis power of the Spirit to speak.

Prompt

Are you generally more apt to follow your own "wisdom" (or that of someone you know or even the crowd's), or is it your habit to pause and look heavenward, asking God for dunamis wisdom of the Spirit? If God's wisdom is different than your own, which have you followed more often? Why? Write it here.

My Breakthrough Prayer for Today

God, clear away any roadblocks of my own assumptions in order that the miraculous open road of your dunamis-filled wisdom may be revealed before me. Amen.

Or craft your own breakthrough prayer below.

Prayer-Hold (to pray throughout today)

God's wisdom, not mine . . .

Like the phoenix rising from the ashes, we too can rise as we discover God's ways of being in a world driven by doing.
—Juanita Rasmus

Day 14: Everything We Need

His divine power [dunamis] has given us everything we need for a godly life through our knowledge of him who called us by his own glory and goodness.
—2 Peter 1:3

Insight

In today's scripture, Peter recaps dunamis as the gift of "everything we need for a godly life" through knowing Christ. The Greek word *zoe* used in this verse, translated into English as "life," specifically refers to the soul and spirit within us. Peter reminds us that though earthly life is frequently physically and emotionally difficult, we have already been provided the resurrection strength and spiritual resources to prevail as we follow Jesus. Scripture assures us that God has already given us everything we need to spiritually thrive and overcome our problems through the Spirit's dunamis power.

Spirit-fostered growth and maturity within is never accomplished through our self-attempts to measure up to what we believe are God's standards or by frequently seeking out emotionally charged spiritual experiences for inspiration. God uses the repeated failures of our own efforts and resulting sense of self-defeat and disillusionment to prepare our hearts to receive the "everything" of dunamis power that alone fosters Kingdom-style faith and growth within us.

How do you know when you're living into the "everything" of the Spirit's dunamis? Paul explains the evidence that will emerge upon the landscape of your life in Galatians 5:22–23 as what he called the fruit of the Holy Spirit that will blossom within us: love, joy, peace, patience, gentleness, kindness, faithfulness, self-control. This prevailing, overcoming fruit of dunamis manifested in you cannot be self-generated. It comes as the result of embracing the maturing gift of new life in Christ to which you have been called.

Prompt

Can you remember any life moment in which you felt God's dunamis had not provided you "everything you need for a godly life" after all? What did it seem to you was specifically missing right then? Reflect further about what played out afterward. What had God's power actually provided you, if not what you had felt you needed? Write it here.

My Breakthrough Prayer for Today

God, dismantle my attitude that material blessings represent your "everything"—so that the glorious reality of what you mean by "everything" may flood through me. Amen.

Or craft your own breakthrough prayer below.

Prayer-Hold (to pray throughout today)

Everything needed . . .

The troubling reality is that believers can be deeply committed to being Christian without ever being deeply formed by Christ.
—Rich Villodas

Day 15: Through Our Words

My message and my preaching were not with wise and persuasive words,
but with a demonstration of the Spirit's power [dunamis], so that your faith
might not rest on human wisdom, but on God's power [dunamis].
—*1 Corinthians 2:4–5*

Insight

In this third week of the guidebook, we will focus on several of the miraculous activities of the Spirit's dunamis that become evident when we commit ourselves to a prayer-fueled life.

In yesterday's scripture, we noted what the apostle Paul named "fruit of the Spirit" and defined them as the outward expressions of increasing spiritual growth (Galatians 5:22–23). Today we consider Paul himself, and how the Spirit's dunamis activity permeated and transformed his natural talents into a potent tool for Kingdom work.

In his previous life before faith conversion, Paul had become a hardcore student of the Jewish law. Acts 22:3 reveals that Paul even studied under Gamaliel, one of the best teachers of the time, who held today's equivalent of a doctorate in law. Biblical scholars assume that Paul, too, reached the same educational status and may have even surpassed his former teacher. With his insatiable quest to learn and his love of debate, Paul was likely fluent in both Hebrew and Greek and possibly other languages. Though he became known as a persecutor of the early Christian movement, Paul was no barbarian without brains.

But after Paul encountered Jesus on the road to Damascus (Acts 9), none of his intellectual accolades mattered anymore. As he grew in faith, prayer, and increasing spiritual maturity, Paul realized he no longer cared about sounding learned or impressing the crowds. He had grown to understand that his own educated, persuasive words intended to convince others intellectually about anything were powerless.

Instead, Paul relied only on the Spirit's dunamis activity to pervade his speech so that God's resurrection power could bring listeners to faith. As Paul increased in spiritual maturity through surrendered prayer asking for the Spirit's dunamis to work through him on behalf of the message and mission of Christ, he was transformed. Pride in his own accomplishments lessened as God's miraculous work moved to center stage for him.

What about you? Do you find yourself striving hard for others to listen to you and to be impressed by your credentials or instead thankful for what the Spirit's dunamis is accomplishing through you?

Prompt

Would you say that your words are often motivated by your emotions (defensiveness, insecurity, superiority, critical of others, desire to be the authority) or do you find yourself holding space for the dunamis of God's Spirit to provide you words and attitude that will bless and encourage others? Write it here.

My Breakthrough Prayer for Today

God, break through my prideful desire to sound capable, talented, or competent in the eyes of others, so that I might live today surrendered to your Spirit's power flowing through my words and actions instead. Amen.

Or craft your own breakthrough prayer below.

Prayer-Hold (to pray throughout today)

Not words, but power . . .

A whole lot of what we call "struggling" is simply delayed obedience.
—*Elisabeth Elliot*

Day 16: For Eternal Life

By his power [dunamis] God raised the Lord from the dead, and he will raise us also.
—1 Corinthians 6:14

One of the surest demonstrations of the Holy Spirit is the power to bring death back to life. The same resurrection power's potency, displayed when God raised Jesus from the grave, continues today. Marriages, friendships, work situations, family dynamics—realities that feel, act, and look dead can be miraculously raised through God's resurrection power attached to our prayers.

God's resurrection dunamis is specifically active in every follower of Christ through Jesus' promise of eternal life. What we know of life on earth is not all there is! Remember again his statement in John 3:16: "For God so loved the world that he gave his one and only Son, that whoever believes in him shall not perish but have eternal life."

Let's look deeper. In the Greek language of Jesus'day, the word for "eternal" indicated something that would never cease nor have an end. The Greek word Jesus used here, *zoe*, translated into English as "life," actually refers to the life of our soul and spirit. Jesus made it clear that receiving new life in Christ brings with it the Spirit's resurrection power. And so, when our earthly body dies, our soul and spirit continue on, resurrected through God's dunamis, united fully into God's everlasting embrace.

46

God's power transcends time and space. When we die in Christ, we do not move from life to death but from death to life. We, too, will be raised by God's power—just like Jesus.

Prompt

It's been said that in Christ, death is not the final sleep—it's the Great Awakening. Given the resurrection power of the Spirit's dunamis, what does this statement mean to you? Write it here.

My Breakthrough Prayer for Today

God, may your Sprit's resurrection-strength power bring new life to the following situations or circumstances that seem "dead" (name them here). Amen.

Or craft your own breakthrough prayer below.

Prayer-Hold (to pray throughout today)

From death to life . . .

The necessary lens that shapes our thinking about life requires us to remove the artificial division between life here on earth and life eternal. Jesus's message in all four Gospels is that the kingdom of heaven is here now.
—Arthur Jones

Day 17: Faith Focus

I want to know Christ—yes, to know the power [dunamis] of his resurrection and participation in his sufferings, becoming like him in his death.
—Philippians 3:10

Insight

Are you a person who needs a to-do list to keep you on track? Or maybe you like to make resolutions for yourself every New Year's Day. Perhaps you keep a bucket list of what you want to experience or accomplish in the future—and when you do, you post photos on social media for all to see. Or you may be wired differently, and it's difficult for you to come up with goals. Possibly you'd like to have a few, and maybe subconsciously you do, but you do not verbalize them for the world to hear.

The apostle Paul's lifelong goal was simple and straightforward: "I want to know Christ." Paul had a singular focus from which he did not deviate, no matter what was taking place around him within the early church or with his own persecution. Paul knew that dunamis power was found in the only person who had been resurrected from the dead: Jesus. He held on to the promise we all have—that we, too, will experience miraculous resurrection from earthly physical death to everlasting life of soul and spirit—but along the way, like Christ, we will all experience suffering.

When Jesus prayed near the end of his life on earth in the Garden of Gethsemane, it was a prayer of surrendered single focus: "God, not my will but yours be done." From a prison cell, Paul wrote in his letter to the Philippians, "I want to know Christ." Paul recognized that the path of suffering for a Christ follower is a tool for the Spirit's dunamis to shape and mature us spiritually. Through loss, rejection, criticism, physical illness, or other venues of challenge, any self-serving priorities of money, prestige, or possessions get stripped away. What is most spiritually valuable and important rises to the top.

If your path of faith includes seasons of difficulty, share this confidence of Jesus, of Paul, and of the "great cloud of witnesses" surrounding you (Hebrews 12:1). Be assured that the provision of the Spirit's miraculous power is the unquenchable source to perfect and mature your faith focus in and through every chapter of your life.

Prompt

What sometimes competes with your faith in Christ for your focus of time, energy, and priority right now? Think back about an occasion when you experienced suffering (health issues, relationship frustrations, financial need, or other crises). Did your faith focus strengthen as you navigated through and, if so, in what way? Write it here.

My Breakthrough Prayer for Today

God, may your resurrection power break through to bring new faith focus and meaning to me in the midst of this season and also in the season of life for those I name now . . . Amen.

Or craft your own breakthrough prayer below.

Prayer-Hold (to pray throughout today)

I want to know Christ . . .

When a train goes through a tunnel and it gets dark, you don't throw away the ticket and jump off. You sit still and trust the engineer.
—*Corrie ten Boom*

Day 18: A New Spirit

For God has not given us a spirit of fear, but of power [dunamis] and of love
and of a sound mind.
—2 Timothy 1:7 NKJV

Insight

In his relationship with his young protégé Timothy, Paul modeled what it looked like to live out of a spirit of power not a spirit of fear.

Paul had every reason to live out of a spirit of fear. His second of two letters to Timothy (the book of the Bible called 2 Timothy) was written from a dark and damp Roman prison cell, just before Paul's death. The Roman emperor Nero had residents in an uproar and nearly burned down half the city of Rome. Christians became a convenient target for Nero, who used them as scapegoats. Paul was one of those caught up in the persecution and was beheaded by Roman officials soon after writing this second letter of pastoral advice.

Timothy had been a faithful servant to Paul since leaving home to become a co-missionary with him more than a decade earlier. Their relationship was almost like one between a father and son. If you're a movie enthusiast, picture *The Karate Kid*'s Mr. Miyagi and Daniel-san; *Star Wars* fans might remember Luke Skywalker and Obi-Wan Kenobi; or if you're into the *Rocky* movies, it's like the relationship between Mickey and Rocky.

From his jail cell, Paul taught and encouraged Timothy as Timothy ministered to the church in Ephesus. His words were bold, even while facing his own impending death. He cautioned Timothy to stay aware that any threatening spirit of fear does not come from the Almighty. His instruction was instead to embrace the blessings bestowed through the Holy Spirit: dunamis power, God's unselfish (*agape*) love, and a sound mind of faith. History reflects that the Spirit's activity through Paul and Timothy's lifestyles of selfless love and self-disciplined minds enabled them to both demonstrate and proclaim God's story to the world. They each chose not to allow fear or discouragement to triumph, to consume their focus, or otherwise to unintentionally limit what was possible.

Prompt

How easily do you open yourself to a spirit of fear—and when you do, to what extent does it affect your ability to selflessly love others or to maintain a sound mind of faith? Write it here.

My Breakthrough Prayer for Today

God, I say no to all fear and yes to your dunamis power, selfless love, and sound mind of faith. Amen.

Or craft your own breakthrough prayer below.

Prayer-Hold (to pray throughout today)

Power, love, and a sound mind . . .

Is the prayer of my lips really the prayer of my life?
—Andrew Murray

Day 19: Through Scripture

Jesus replied [to the Sadducees], "You are in error because you do not know the Scriptures or the power [dunamis] of God."
—Matthew 22:29

Insight

When we read about the dunamis power of God in scripture, it's often in context of the Spirit's activity available or active in and through the lives of those who follow Christ. However, in today's passage, the Sadducees, educated religious dignitaries of Jesus' day, have tried to trap Jesus in an argument. One of the beliefs the Sadducees held was that there is no resurrection of the dead. Sadducees even rejected the spiritual realm and anything having to do with the angelic and demonic. They prided themselves instead as a religious and political sect comprised of priests, striving in their self-righteousness to be a people of influence.

If Jesus were present in physical body right now where we are today, would he find Christians who pride themselves on being moral people doing good works but lacking when it comes to actual faith? For some, "Christianity" may be more like an outer garment to wear for appearance rather than an "all-in" relationship with Jesus taking root in their hearts. And like the Sadducees, many Christians today passively deny or ignore the reality of the spiritual realm alive with the Spirit's dunamis, viewing it as something that occurred during a time long ago. It's no wonder that Christianity is considered by many to have become powerless.

When Jesus answered the Sadducees in this account recorded by Matthew, he first pointed out that they didn't know the scriptures or the dunamis power of God. What a clear, specific way Jesus had of identifying the two components required to shift "faith" from moral self-righteous behavior to a miracle-filled adventure following him!

How well do you personally know both the Scriptures and the dunamis of God's Spirit moving and active in and through you? Reading and reflecting on God's word (scripture) is essential. It's not only for information but also sets the stage for our spiritual transformation when it's paired with breakthrough prayer asking for the Spirit's dunamis-fueled possibilities to open before you. These are your primary tools to move beyond only intellectual affirmation of your faith into a living vibrant lifestyle that will open you ever further to the Spirit's explosive power.

Prompt

What did you see, feel, experience, and realize as you read about the Sadducees and Jesus' response to them? What might Jesus say to you now? Write it here.

My Breakthrough Prayer for Today

God, rouse me from my "spiritual sleep" as I read your scripture, so that I am spiritually awake and prayerfully alert to what your Spirit's dunamis longs to do in and through me. Amen.

Or craft your own breakthrough prayer below.

Prayer-Hold (to pray throughout today)

Scripture plus the power of God . . .

Do not have your concert first, and then tune your instrument afterwards. Begin the day with the Word of God and prayer, and get first of all into harmony with [Christ].

—Hudson Taylor

Day 20: The Cross

For the message of the cross is foolishness to those who are perishing, but to us who are being saved it is the power [dunamis] of God.
—1 Corinthians 1:18

Insight

Necklaces, earrings, bracelets, rings, T-shirts, and tattoos featuring the cross upon which Jesus was crucified are popular attire across all age groups in our country. Some see wearing the symbol of the cross as a gratitude-filled representation of our forgiven new life empowered by the Spirit's miraculous dunamis activity for a future of hope and possibility. Others might like the cross symbolism for completely different reasons.

However, the symbol of the cross had a very unique meaning during Jesus' time on earth: death, by the most excruciating means. To make it as humiliating as possible, criminals were required to carry their own crosses to their executions.

Jesus told his disciples ahead of time, "Whoever wants to be my disciple must deny themselves and take up their cross and follow me. For whoever wants to save their life will lose it, but whoever loses their life for me will find it. What good will it be for someone to gain the whole world, yet forfeit their soul?" (Matthew 16:24–26) Jesus' phrase, "take up your cross," was and is an invitation to total surrender, dying to your old self in order to receive Christ's new life and to follow him completely—through earthly death and into everlasting life. Saying yes to this invitation requires submitting to what you know to be Christ's priorities (rather than your own wants and preferences) in every aspect of your time, money, relationships, possessions, and plans. Be assured that the return will be unparalleled.

Next time you wear (or see) the symbol of the cross, ask yourself whether you are viewing it as a representation of blessings you desire or have received from the Almighty—or whether it symbolizes your own relentless decision to actively keep surrendering all as you follow Jesus. The real message of the cross is indeed foolishness to those without faith or to those whose prevailing pursuit is to reduce stress and live pain-free, self-focused, carefree lives. But for those who have said yes to Jesus' invitation, you'll experience daily the message of the cross through the resurrection-strength dunamis activity of God's Spirit that resources and makes all things possible.

Prompt

When you see the symbol of the cross (in jewelry, on clothing, in church), what comes to your mind first: the blessings God has given you? Or do you see the cross as an invitation to your own spiritual surrender, with prayer requesting breakthroughs that will set you free to more fully follow Jesus? Or something else? Write it here.

My Breakthrough Prayer for Today

God, open every door of my mind and heart that I've kept tightly closed or barricaded by my own self-interests, fears, or procrastination. May the dunamis activity of your Spirit break through, fill, and transform me completely as I follow you fully. Amen.

Or craft your own breakthrough prayer below.

Prayer-Hold (to pray throughout today)

The message is power . . .

There are no crown-bearers in heaven who were not cross-bearers here below.
—Charles Spurgeon

Day 21: War Cry

*And lead us not into temptation, but deliver us from the evil one. For Yours
is the kingdom and the power[dunamis] and the glory forever. Amen.*
—Matthew 6:13 NKJV

Insight

Certain songs just get stuck in your head. If you're a parent, you
might find yourself singing nursery rhymes or the theme songs of
children's shows you've memorized through the sheer repetition of
hearing them. Sometimes with those songs stuck in your head, you
begin to think about the words differently and realize the message
the song is actually communicating to you.

This also happens when we choose to immerse ourselves in
scripture. Perhaps you have occasions day-to-day when the dunamis
activity of the Holy Spirit might bring to mind a familiar verse or
passage for the purpose of bringing you encouragement in a situation.
Such a passage or verse may even become your shield and strength
in spiritual battle.

Since early in its history, the church of Jesus Christ has universally
used the prayer Jesus taught his disciples (found in Matthew 6:9–13)
that we refer to as the Lord's Prayer. It's memorized by both children
and adults and affirms the dunamis power and kingship of God
forever as our miraculous source. In fact, Matthew 6:13 is more than
the final sentence of the prayer. It's a declaration, our "war cry" of
God's ultimate power and victory!

Christ promises us an abundant new life following him, as he
described in John 10:10—and he didn't mean just a "getting by" type
of experience. Repeat today's scripture as your spiritually victorious

war cry whenever you need to affirm that the dunamis activity of God's kingdom can overcome that which might seem insurmountable within you (fear, anxiety, brokenness, discouragement, weariness, fatigue) or before you (problems, challenges, disappointments, changes).

Prompt

Is there a scripture or verse from the Bible that often comes to your mind or that has ever been like a spiritual shield or war cry for you? Note it here—or if you'd like to choose today's verse (or any other) to use for this, note it here as well. Write it here.

My Breakthrough Prayer for Today

God, shatter any fatigue, weariness, or anything else that seems insurmountable in my faith, and surge through my spirit anew with a war cry celebrating your miraculous kingdom and dunamis power! Amen.

Or craft your own breakthrough prayer below.

Prayer-Hold (to pray throughout today)

Yours is the Kingdom and the power . . .

There is an immaterial world, a spiritual reality, that we can begin to understand only by faith. The Holy Spirit gives us access to an entirely different level of understanding.
—Len Wilson

Day 22: Not Ashamed

*For I am not ashamed of the gospel, because it is the power [dunamis] of
God that brings salvation to everyone who believes: first to the Jew, then to
the Gentile.*
—*Romans 1:16*

Insight

Our final week's theme involves how to assume a "spiritual
posture" that opens your best capacity to become a vessel for the
Spirit's dunamis working in and through you. We begin first with the
spiritual posture of our boldness.

According to *Christianity Today* magazine, Nigeria is one of
the top fifteen most dangerous countries in the world in which to
follow Jesus. On Christmas Eve 2020, Islamic terrorists raided a
small Nigerian village and abducted Christian pastor Bulus Yikura.
He was held for ransom for two months, and his captors announced
he would be executed if it was not paid. The terrifying story broke
quickly and circulated across the world's media outlets.

When forced to make hostage videos, Pastor Yikura turned his
on-camera time into an opportunity to share his Christian testimony.
Miraculously, only a few hours before the scheduled execution for his
faith, he received the unexpected news he had been freed and was
returned to his grateful family.

Pastor Yikura echoed the words of the apostle Paul in his hostage
testimony: he was not ashamed of the gospel because of its power
(dunamis) to bring salvation to everyone who believes. Paul wrote

the book of Romans and most of his New Testament letters while awaiting trial then, ultimately, while on death row. Both Paul and Pastor Yikura knew and personally experienced the dunamis of God. This power helped them face death with supernatural grace and also speak the good news of Jesus boldly.

Remember, as a follower of Christ you also have the Spirit's same dunamis! No need to be ashamed of the gospel, to be fearful of honestly sharing your God stories with others, or taking courageous steps of faith. The unashamed witness of your faith and breakthrough prayers has a ripple effect. It's multiplied by the Spirit far beyond what you will ever know—spanning out over time and into other lives that need redemption, healing, and hope.

Prompt

Are those around you (friends, family, coworkers, neighbors, and others) aware of your faith in Christ and that you believe prayer makes a difference? If yes, is this because you have shared stories about how God has led, guided, or provided for you, or have you shared stories about answered prayers with them? Knowing you attend church is not the same as knowing about your faith. Write it here.

My Own Breakthrough Prayer for Today

God, break through my hesitancy and grant me your Spirit's dunamis boldness in moments when I want to shy away from sharing my story of faith in you with others, or about your answers to my prayers. Amen.

Or craft your own breakthrough prayer below.

Prayer-Hold (to pray throughout today)

I am not ashamed . . .

Resolution One: I will live for God.
Resolution Two: If no one else does, I still will.
—Jonathan Edwards

Day 23: Servant vs. Volunteer

I became a servant of this gospel by the gift of God's grace given me through the working of his power [dunamis].
—Ephesians 3:7

Insight

Over and over in his writings, the apostle Paul called himself a servant. And he was clear that the duties he performed as a servant of Christ were not by his own human power but through God's dunamis at work.

The Greek word that's translated as "servant" in today's verse was used in Paul's time to reference someone who carried out the commands and desires of their master, and Paul knew he served the greatest Master of all. For this reason, Paul viewed all his time and resources to be at the divine discretion of whatever was needed to share and establish the gospel. Paul's was not the behavior of a private citizen donating his time for religious service whenever he had a convenient moment. Instead, Paul served with everything he had, all that he was, always and in all ways trusting the dunamis resurrection power's efficacy to flow through him.

Growing in spiritual maturity is a journey that will inevitably lead you to make Paul's same shift of comprehending what it means to serve the gospel of Christ. It often feels good when volunteering to assist others, to provide food or clothing, or to help build or repair a house for a family. It feels good to give an extra hour at church as a volunteer greeter or to sing in the choir during the worship service. Gifts like these of your available extra time do make a difference. But a Christ follower's genuine identity and orientation is to become a whole-life servant, willing to serve at the pleasure of the heavenly Master whenever so led with all that you have and are. That is what unleashes the Spirit's dunamis through you to a magnitude you never thought possible.

Are you holding back, somehow fearful that God will force you to become a Kingdom workaholic who eventually burns out, neglects your home life, ignores your self-care, and quits your essential daily devotional prayer time? Not a chance. When you recognize that God is the trustworthy steward of your new life in Christ within and you acquiesce to the power of the Holy Spirit, you'll find that the dunamis-powered healthy identity of a servant aligns every aspect of your life with the love and growth-producing priorities of Christ. Rather than hoping for better life "balance," expect the Spirit's dunamis to give your call to serve a beautiful integration of peace, fruitfulness, and love.

Prompt

As you consider the differences between *servant* and *volunteer*, which would likely describe you most accurately at the moment? Or do you vacillate between these two? If so, can you think of specifics? Write it here.

My Breakthrough Prayer for Today

God, remove my strongholds of selfishness so that I may shift to selfless dunamis servanthood for you. Amen.

Or craft your own breakthrough prayer below.

Prayer-Hold (to pray throughout today)

God's power to serve . . .

The way we can give everything of ourselves cheerfully and joyfully to God is if we give out of a heart filled with gratitude for all God has first given us.
—Kent Millard

Day 24: Battle Ready

Finally, be strong in the Lord and in his mighty power [dunamis]. Put on the full armor of God, so that you can take your stand against the devil's schemes. For our struggle is not against flesh and blood, but against the rulers, against the authorities, against the powers of this dark world and against the spiritual forces of evil in the heavenly realms.
—Ephesians 6:10–12

Insight

If you've ever served in the military, you know that all training prepares the recruits for battle regardless of whether they face active combat deployment during their careers. The job of military instructors is to prepare civilians to become battle ready (whether as marines, air force airmen, army soldiers, navy sailors, space force guardians, or coast guardsmen). That's not an easy task to accomplish in only nine to twelve weeks of boot camp! However, those who are willing, ready, and available and who give themselves over to the process will experience transformation. They will become battle ready.

Paul used the imagery of becoming battle-prepared spiritually when he wrote today's scripture message to Christians who desired to grow in their faith. The battles Paul had in mind were against what he named the "schemes of the devil." Jesus called the devil the Father of Lies, our enemy. Satan, the devil, is described in the Bible as the Evil One who masterminds the "forces of darkness" rampant around and against us.

The goal of evil's darkness is to deter, discourage, tempt, and ultimately win over Christ's followers onto a self-serving path of destruction instead. Paul's urgency for Christians was to stay aware and to "put on the whole armor of God" for the purpose of resisting evil's tactics of fear, worry, and distraction, to keep their focus on following Jesus. Read Paul's entire description of the armor of God found in Ephesians 6:10–17 for your awareness and encouragement.

Have you ever felt like you have been in a spiritual battle, that your back is against the wall and the Evil One has you surrounded? You may still feel battle-fatigued and tired. Paul's image in Ephesians 6 is a reminder that we are like soldiers going into spiritual battle. The only way to declare victory is by standing strong in the Lord's mighty dunamis power. Ask God for spiritual stubbornness and remember to keep surrendering to the dunamis of God's Spirit that can and will prevail.

Prompt

Jesus stayed spiritually battle ready, and we can too. Look carefully through Ephesians 6:10–17. What part(s) of the armor of God do you need to focus on grasping and putting into place in your faith? Write it here.

My Breakthrough Prayer for Today

God, dispel my casual attitude about following Jesus, and may your Spirit's dunamis motivate me to enlist in whatever spiritual training I need to become battle ready on your behalf. Amen.

Or craft your own breakthrough prayer below.

Prayer-Hold (to pray throughout today)

Be strong in the Lord . . .

As long as we let the Word of God be our only armor, we can look confidently into the future.
—Dietrich Bonhoeffer

Day 25: Race-Prepared

. . . being strengthened with all power [dunamis] according to his glorious might, so that you may have great endurance and patience.
—Colossians 1:11

Insight

On day 6 of this guidebook, you may remember our focus was on spiritual "wait training." Today's scripture is a verse from a prayer Paul wrote to the Christ followers at the early church at Colossae. His emphasis in prayer was asking for the dunamis of God's spirit to provide them strength that would become evident not just in their willingness to be patient. He also prayed for their endurance, a word in the original Greek that inferred perseverance, steadfastness, and constancy.

Have you ever trained for a race of any kind? Whether you've raced yourself or been a spectator, you've likely observed that when competitors run, they must rely on their preparation and training to keep their pace. Poor prerace training means it's evident on race day who did not adequately prepare. Even racers who have prepared often try to run alongside a "pacer" who has trained well because it helps them match another's steady pace and perform to the best of their ability.

Remember the spiritual race description found in Hebrews 12:1–2: "Therefore, since we are surrounded by such a great cloud of witnesses, let us throw off everything that hinders and the sin that so easily entangles. And let us run with perseverance the race marked out for us, fixing our eyes on Jesus, the pioneer and perfecter of faith."

Patient perseverance, when you surrender to preparation by God's supernatural dunamis, allows you to run the race or path set before you equipped with the spiritual endurance it will require. Thankfully, you can always keep your eyes on Jesus as your pacer.

Prompt

Have you ever heard the expression that you should run your spiritual race "at the pace of God's grace"? As you reflect on this statement, what meaning or encouragement do you find in it? Write it here.

My Breakthrough Prayer for Today

God, break through any lack of spiritual self-discipline in me so that a new willingness to develop spiritual endurance unfolds. Amen.

Or craft your own breakthrough prayer below.

Prayer-Hold (to pray throughout today)

Dunamis endurance and patience . . .

It is not prayer that is strenuous, but the overcoming of our own laziness.
—Oswald Chambers

Day 26: My Weakness

But he said to me, "My grace is sufficient for you, for my power [dunamis] is made perfect in weakness." Therefore I will boast all the more gladly about my weaknesses, so that Christ's power [dunamis] may rest on me. That is why, for Christ's sake, I delight in weaknesses, in insults, in hardships, in persecutions, in difficulties. For when I am weak, then I am strong.
—2 Corinthians 12:9–10

Insight

Hudson Taylor, British Christian missionary and eventual founder of the China Inland Mission, followed God's call at age twenty-one to a country and people who knew little of, and did not welcome, the good news of Jesus. Like the apostle Paul, Taylor became known for placing ongoing prayer as primary and asking the Spirit to unleash breakthrough dunamis power in and through every circumstance and need. When he died in 1905 after fifty-one years in China, he left a legacy there of eighteen thousand Christian conversions plus an active working team of eight hundred missionaries across that country.

This inspiring track record of service was accomplished through a lifetime that also brimmed with personal challenges including repeated illness and physical breakdowns, catastrophes, disasters, bereavements, rejection, plus periodic lack of financial resources and shortage of fellow workers. How could such missionary effectiveness have been possible? Taylor once remarked to a friend that his greatest spiritual blessings had come to him in association with his various sicknesses or as direct spiritual fruitfulness of some physical breakdown through which he had been called to pass.

Reread today's scripture verses and reflect again upon Paul's explanation. Whenever and in whatever ways you are humanly weak, God uses those as a venue through which to flow supernatural power so that in your weakness you are made strong. Occasions of hardship are the ideal opportunity for God's power to do something extraordinary in and through you. Think now about any difficulties or challenges you may be facing and whether you have considered them to be roadblocks or whether, like Paul and Hudson Taylor, you might better shift to view them as venues for spiritual blessings by the power of God's dunamis.

Prompt

In what areas do you feel the most weak or vulnerable? Name these to God and ask for the Spirit's dunamis power to do, work, and accomplish beyond what you can manage yourself. Write it here.

My Breakthrough Prayer for Today

God, reform my view of any personal discouragement or failing so that I may instead see it as a window through which your dunamis resurrection strength and power can shine through. Amen.

Or craft your own breakthrough prayer below.

Prayer-Hold (to pray throughout today)

Where I am weak, God is strong.

The Holy Spirit is always at work in the world and in the church regardless of the problems that we face and regardless of the darkness that seems to prevail.
—Pete Bellini

Day 27: Capacity for Hope

May the God of hope fill you with all joy and peace as you trust in him, so that you may overflow with hope by the power [dunamis] of the Holy Spirit.
—Romans 15:13

Insight

It's possible to develop a "scarcity mentality" without even being aware of it—even if you're a Christian. Before you know it, you can fall into the habit of always thinking or commenting about what's missing, what you or others don't have enough of, or how there's never enough of something to go around. A scarcity mentality can even permeate your faith life when you begin to consistently complain to others that God didn't provide enough or do enough according to what you requested. Eventually, a spiritual scarcity mentality adversely affects your view of the Almighty's power, so that your faith feels hopeless. Then your hopelessness begins to influence and negatively reproduce in the faith of those around you.

In today's scripture, Paul expressed the actual truth about the generous nature of the Spirit's dunamis power in his life and ministry. He had personally experienced its miraculous activity of abundance repeatedly in difficult circumstances that had featured scarcities of safety, food, support, friendship, and finances. No spiritual scarcity mentality for Paul!

Instead, Paul described our God of hope and expectation as capable of filling us completely to the brim, to full measure—as the original Greek word he used inferred—with joy and peace even as we confidently trust forward for God's provision. Paul added that that the result of our trust, through the Spirit's dunamis, is that we will overflow with the miraculous power of hope. The dunamis power of hope will spill over from us, splash around us onto everything and everyone through our words and behavior. Hope comes not from deciding we have enough but rather through the expectation that God, who always provides more than we can ask, think, or imagine, will supply what matters most to Christ's divine purposes through us.

Prompt

Would you say you assert more of a scarcity mentality or a hope mentality when it comes to how you view what's happening to you and others? Write it here.

My Breakthrough Prayer for Today

God, break through my self-serving desires and requests for blessings. May I find freedom to allow you to fill me to overflowing with hope and expectation for your abundant provision. Amen.

Or craft your own breakthrough prayer below.

Prayer-Hold (to pray throughout today)

Overflow with hope . . .

God is the only one who can make the valley of trouble a door of hope.
—Catherine Marshall

Day 28: Sustenance

The Son is the radiance of God's glory and the exact representation of his being, sustaining all things by his powerful [dunamis] word. After he had provided purification for sins, he sat down at the right hand of the Majesty in heaven.
—Hebrews 1:3

Insight

Social media is the typical go-to location where celebratory photos of newborns are posted—often with comments of newsworthy observation that the tiny miracle "looks just like" Dad, Mom, or another relative. Have you ever been told you resemble one of your parents or perhaps that one of your own children is the very picture of you?

The author of the book of Hebrews took the same approach by explaining in today's scripture that "The Son is the . . . exact representation of [God's] being." In the original Greek language as it was written, the word translated into English as "exact representation" was frequently used back in that day to describe carving, stamping, or engraving an exact image. The author wanted us to understand that Christ's family resemblance to God the Father is precise. And if the new life of Christ is alive in us, we carry that family lineage as well. As we surrender through prayer, the dunamis of God's Spirit is at work maturing and chiseling away old behaviors, priorities, and thinking that are not of Christ's likeness, so that we might also shine with God's radiance. This is the journey of faith!

Look again at today's scripture. It also holds a note of reassurance for moments when you may feel weary or discouraged, uncertain whether you are progressing in your spiritual growth. It is through the dunamis power of the Spirit that everything is "sustained"—the Greek word originally used also translates into English as "to uphold, to carry the burden, to be moved forward." Even when you feel incapable or unable, the Spirit's dunamis is upholding you, carrying you, and working in and through you beyond what you can imagine. This is a miraculous aspect of our family DNA in Christ Jesus.

As you conclude this 28-day breakthrough prayer guidebook experiment, may you continue your daily practices of…

- reading and reflecting on scripture,
- praying, asking God to break through anew, opening doors of new possibilities and spiritual growth,
- taking bold steps of surrender and transformation, and
- serving others through demonstrations of Christ's selfless love.

And the best part ? As you continue these practices, through the sustenance of the Spirit's dunamis, your family likeness to Jesus will increasingly emerge. Christlikeness in you shines not by imitation but by inhabitation. Let the Spirit's dunamis power inhabit you completely!

Prompt

As you consider the degree of your hunger to mature more into your family resemblance to Jesus, what could set the stage for a frequent closer and more personal encounter with God than you have practiced up until now? Write it here.

My Breakthrough Prayer for Today

God, demolish my tendency to ignore your living presence in every detail of my life and fill me anew with an attitude of welcome and openness to your Spirit of dunamis. Amen.

Or craft your own breakthrough prayer below.

Prayer-Hold (to pray throughout today)

God is my sustainer . . .

Christian formation is not simply a matter of internalizing the words of the Bible. For true formation to happen, we must encounter Christ ever more deeply through the power of the Holy Spirit.
—David Watson

Continuing Your Journey

Twenty-eight days of experiencing how the Holy Spirit can break through to give you a more powerful life! Congratulations!

But this 28-day experiment with breakthrough prayer is not the end—it has only been the beginning:

- the beginning of a new season of following Christ with awareness of and surrender to God's miraculous resurrection power, active in every aspect of both your practical and spiritual life

- the beginning of a deeper personal acquaintanceship with the Holy Spirit so that you may continue to advance in recognizing the Spirit's activity and leading

- the start (or strengthening) of your practice adding breakthrough prayer to your daily communications with God and allow the "dynamite" of the Spirit's dunamis to transform you and your circumstances

- the new habit of incorporating prayer-holds from scripture throughout your day to help yourself stay spiritually focused up and out on the Almighty, not only down and in on your own desires and agenda

And now, this *Dyanmite Prayer* guidebook with notes from your own day-to-day reflections and breakthrough prayers can become your dunamis lifelong prayer guide. Whenever you feel the need to become more battle ready, for example, you can go to the table of contents to guide you to that day's entry, breakthrough prayer, and prayer-hold to refresh you, to reconnect with the dunamis of God's wisdom, to refocus on what it means to serve, or whatever you need.

Check out more resources, stories, and ideas for engaging in a deeper and more meaningful prayer life at dynamiteprayer.com and post your own stories of God's miraculous intervention in your life to share with and inspire others!

And, as always, reach out to us anytime. We are praying for you and would love to pray with you in person or on behalf of whatever is on your heart.

Rosario Picardo (rpicardo@united.edu)

Sue Nilson Kibbey (snkibbey@united.edu)

Afterword

In the Foreword to this devotional book Dr. Rosario Picardo described the breakthrough prayer visioning retreat at United Theological Seminary, which was led by Rev. Sue Nilson Kibbey. Rev. Kibbey encouraged all the retreat participants to pray the following breakthrough prayer daily for six weeks before our retreat in February 2020: "Miraculous God of breakthroughs, speak, show, and inspire us where your spirit is leading next for United. Open doors that will usher in a new season of creativity, faithfulness, and fruitfulness in the name of Jesus. And together grant us boldness, courage, and power without limits to step through the doors you open. In Christ's name. Amen."

We encouraged about ninety trustees, faculty, students, alumni, and staff to pray this prayer daily before the retreat.

Basically, we were asking God through the Holy Spirit to lead us in realizing it is not about what any of us want individually but what God wants us to do in the future: "Not my will, but thine be done."

And God has been faithful in continuing to answer that breakthrough prayer.

One of the ideas that came through the retreat was that God would open new doors to partnerships with other faith-based groups for seminary educational programs which met the needs of the faith-based organization.

And God has been faithful in answering that prayer. Since our "not my will but thine be done" retreat in 2020, God inspired us to develop Houses of Study to appeal to specific needs: the Fresh Expressions House of Study, the Mosaix House of Study to develop multiracial congregations, a Hispanic House of Study with all classes in Spanish, a Pentecostal House of Study, and a Global Wesleyan House of Study with other potential houses of study on the drawing board.

Furthermore, God opened new doors of generosity to provide for the establishment of The Bishop Bruce Ough Innovation Center at United under the inspiring and innovative leadership of Rev. Sue Nilson Kibbey. The Innovation Center enables us to provide spiritual renewal experiences for pastors and congregations of many denominations all over the nation led by Rev. Kibbey.

We had been praying that God would enable us to become debt free by our 150th Jubilee celebration in October 2021. The final gifts came in the summer of 2021, and we were able to burn the $4 million mortgage on our facilities. Thanks be to God.

Furthermore, God has opened new doors of generosity with unexpected gifts for scholarships for our students. A foundation that chooses to remain anonymous that we had never heard about contacted us to discuss a proposal to give us $1 million to establish an academic dean's half or full tuition scholarship for exceptional students. Later this same foundation gave us a $2 million Jubilee gift in honor of our 150th anniversary celebration. This Jubilee gift is designated to reduce the educational indebtedness of all our students who graduate in the 2022 academic year by $20,000 each. This means that 30 percent of our nearly one hundred graduates this year will graduate debt free.

God is so faithful to us and continues to bless us with new students and the scholarship support needed to enable them to graduate with less educational indebtedness.

Frequently, we focus on what we want and ask God to give it to us. However, a breakthrough prayer initiative is surrendering ourselves into the hands of God, praying like Jesus—"not my will but thine be done"—and trusting God to lead us into the future in ways we could not have anticipated.

Thanks be to God.

Grace and Peace,

Dr. Kent Millard, President

United Theological Seminary

Dayton, Ohio

Printed in the USA
CPSIA information can be obtained
at www.ICGtesting.com
CBHW020342040224
3980CB00004B/24

9 781953 495365